A QUICK GUIDE TO eBook PUBLISHING

The kindle way

RONKE ADERINBOYE

ISBN: 9798700741156

DEDICATION

This book is dedicated to all those who desire to kindle the light in the dark, illuminating the path of men through writing and publishing.

Ronke Aderinboye

ACKNOWLEDGMENT

The unwavering efforts of Mr. Solomon Okpa, Ogapatapata as widely known, in encouraging the writing and publishing of this book is sincerely acknowledged and appreciated.

CONTENTS

INTRODUCTION

This book is a guide on how to get your manuscript published on Amazon using basic and advanced methods. Amazon is an electronic book publishing company founded in 2007 and has the headquarters located in Seattle, Washington, United States of America. Publishing books on Amazon requires navigating through the kindle direct publishing (kdp) platform. The kdp platform provides the writer great wealth of opportunities. kindle direct publishing provides authors the advantage to self-publish at no cost. Authors can publish both eBooks and paperbacks (hard copy books) on kdp at free cost. Books can be published within few minutes using kindle direct publishing and it can come alive on the kindle store within 72 hours. Authors have copyrights to their books, set book prices and get royalties on book sales. Are you a writer? Have you wondered how to get your books published? Then this guide is for you. Getting your manuscripts published as electronic books could give them wide readership and at the same time earn you royalties. Electronic books otherwise known as eBooks, are books in digital form which comprises texts, images or both and are readable on the flat-panel display of computers or other electronic devices. With advancement in technology and the widespread of internet users, delivering books in electronic form could be a way for an author to becoming a bestseller. Creating eBooks is like building an edifice and it entails putting the raw manuscript in proper shape to make it fit for publication. This book will help you with steps to formatting your manuscript, getting a kdp account, designing your covers, getting an International Standard Book Number (ISBN) and other relevant steps to eBook publishing on Amazon.

Learners' guide to eBook Publishing

1 BOOK STRUCTURE

Creating your eBook starts from the process of using Microsoft Word to build your document. The document to be formatted for conversion to eBook should have standard sections such as the cover page, copyright segment, dedication page, acknowledgement page, forward, preface, table of content page, introduction, the body or chapters and back page. The order of pages that appear after the copyright page and before the introduction and chapter pages, are not inviolable and can be altered, but all sections are necessary contents for publishing a good book. The different sections are briefly discussed.

i. **Cover page**: This is the first part you see of a book. It is the first point of attraction of a book to the reader. The cover page carries the book title, subtitle and author's name.

ii. **Copyright page**: This is the protection ownership right to the contents of the book. It carries information on copyright, publisher details, the international standard book number (ISBN) and Library of Congress number. The information written in the copyright page gives the extent of content usage allowed by others and the details of who to contact before usage. Lifting contents from a book and using them without permission is an abuse of copyright which is termed "plagiarism." Copyright abuse is a criminal offense punishable by law.

iii.   **Dedication page**: This section is optional and its inclusion in a book depends on author's choice. It is a page containing the name of person or persons to whom the author dedicates the book to, in honor. It is normally written in one or two sentences.

iv.   **Acknowledgement**: This page contains the author's appreciation of all assistance provided in the process of the book creation. This page is normally not more than a page.

v.   **Foreword:** This page contains an introduction on the book given by a person other than the author. This page is signed by the person who has written it.

vi.   **Table of contents**: This page lists out all the different sections in the book along with the corresponding pages as they appear in the book, inclusive of the table of content page. It serves as a quick guide to navigate through the book. The table of contents does not include the title page and copyright page.

vii.   **Preface**: This page is written and signed by the author. It gives information on conception of the book and recognition to those who have assisted in the writing process. Where acknowledgement has been given in the preface, a separate acknowledgement page will not be necessary. Dedication, acknowledgement, forward, preface, are all meant to boost perception of the book.

viii.   **Introduction**: This contains the author's overview of the book contents, which the reader expects to get in details by reading the book. This is best written after the whole book interior content has been created.

ix.   **Body/Chapters:** These are the proceeding sections of the book where contents in the book are organized into parts, with clear headings.

x.   **Back page:** The back page contains author's information referred to as "about the author." It also contains a short description of the book known as blurb, and the ISBN. About the author and blurb could be optional depending on author's choice.

2 DOCUMENT FORMATTING

Document formatting refers to the way a document is laid out on the page. It involves organizing a document to be well laid-out using appropriate font selection, font size, spacing, margins, alignment, columns, indentation and other properties. The practical steps to formatting include:

i. Setting the page and margins

ii. Choosing suitable styles and customizing same

iii. Formatting the interior chapters

iv. Fixing the cover page

v. Inserting pagination

vi. Headers fixation

vii. Extras

viii. Adding images if available

ix. Table of contents arrangement

x. Proof and conversion to PDF

All these formatting steps are done on Microsoft Word with the use of a standard page size. When irregular sizes are used, it may restrict your global book outreach on Amazon. The commonly used paper size is 6" × 9".

Setting the Standard Paper Size

The document intended for conversion to eBook is trimmed to a specific width and height. The standard trim size or paper size used is 6" × 9" or 15.24 × 22.86 cm. This is the common trim size used for eBook publication on Amazon bookshelf. Trimming a manuscript to 6" × 9" involves the following steps:

i. Open the manuscript in Microsoft Word

ii. Click on the Layout tab

iii. Select "Size" option on the page setup menu

iv. Click on the option of "More Paper Sizes" which opens a dialogue box

v. Set the paper size to a width of 6" and a height of 9"

vi. Click 'OK' and save the document.

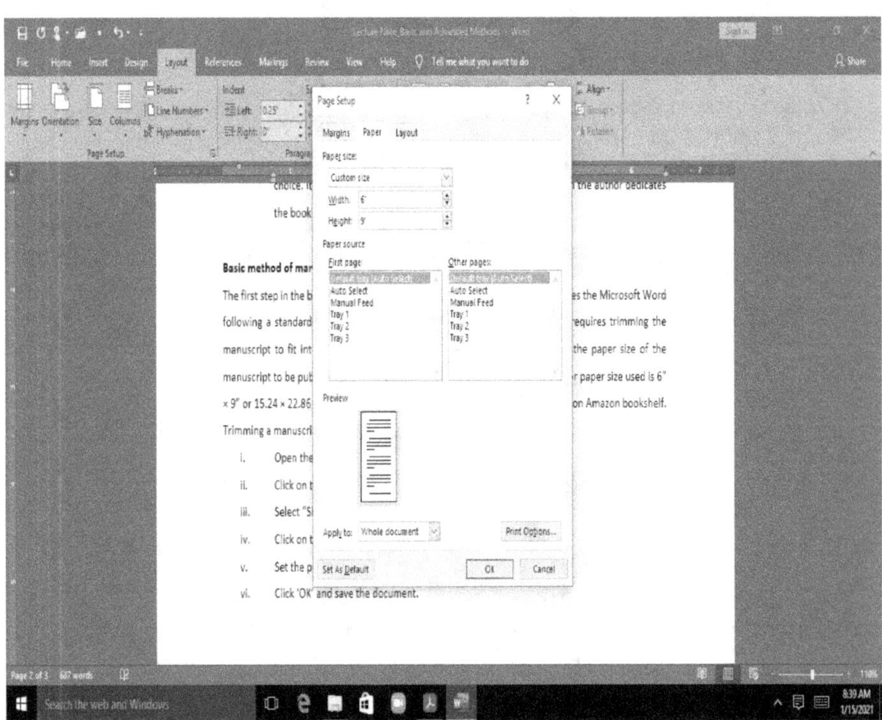

Exercise 1

Set your document to a trim size of 6" × 9".

3 OPTIONS FOR DOCUMENT FORMATTING

1. CreateSpace Formatted Template

A template is a document type that creates a copy of itself when it is opened. A writing template is a guide that a writer follows while writing an article, a book, a letter, etc. A template aims to help the writer follow a specific structure in order to write fast and save tremendous time, especially for beginners. The CreateSpace template is a customized Microsoft Word document that is designed as a yardstick for easy formatting of a document. The use of CreateSpace formatting template is a basic way of document formatting. It involves editing or deleting and replacing the contents of the template with your own manuscript, right from the title page to the last section. The CreateSpace template has been readily formatted to the standard trim size of 6" × 9" commonly used in the United states. However, there are other trim size options. Documents with graphics or images that bleed (i.e., graphics or images that extend to the edge of the page) will require an increased trim size. For the standard trim size of 6" × 9", 0.125" and 0.25" are added to the width and height, respectively for pages with bleed. The CreateSpace template which includes a blank template or a template with sample content is downloadable for use on the Amazon website.

Exercise 2

Format your manuscript using a downloaded CreateSpace formatted template

2. Kindle Create Application

The kindle create application is a free document formatting application launched by Amazon kdp. It provides a simplified and professional method of document formatting compared to the CreateSpace formatting template. It automatically converts manuscripts into kindle eBooks, detects and styles chapter titles. Amazon has moved CreateSpace which is the print-on-demand (paperback) service of Amazon to kindle direct publishing which is the kindle eBook service. The functional site is kdp.amazon.com This merger provides eBooks and print books services on Amazon kindle direct publishing. The kindle create application can be downloaded directly from the kindle direct publishing platform. From your kdp account, download can be done using the *"Get started with kindle content creation tool"* link which is available on the bookshelf page. This link will take you to the kindle tools and resources page. Scroll down to the bottom of the diagram under manuscript formatting resources, click on the link, *"kindle create"*. This link takes you to the Amazon page where you can download the kindle create app. on your computer.

Formatting documents with kindle create app. starts with an unformatted manuscript and finishes with a file that is ready for publication. To format a document with kindle create app.;

- Open the downloaded kindle create application
- Click on the "Choose" icon

- Click on "Choose File". This allows you to choose the documents from stored files. Note that the document to be uploaded for formatting on the kindle create app. should start from the first chapter of the manuscript. There should be no title page, introduction, table of content or preliminary pages included, as these will be inserted in the front matter section and should not appear in the body.

- The selected document file will then be imported and converted. This might take few minutes.

- Once import is successful, click on "Continue" at the top right corner

- Then click on "Get started"

Once your document is well formatted, a table of content is generated which can be accepted or rejected. If "reject" option is selected, it takes you to the page where you can edit the front matter, body and back matter of your book.

- On the "Front matter" tab, click on the "plus +" sign to insert the information on title page, copyright, dedication, table of contents and other front matter related drop-down options. Select and fill as relevant. The table of contents can be done using the insert icon on the top left-hand pane.

- On the "body" tab, click on the "plus +" sign to display the relevant chapters. Note that the document to be uploaded for formatting on the kindle create app. should start from the first chapter of the manuscript. The document should not include title page, introduction, table of content or preliminary pages as these will be inserted in the front matter section and should not appear in the body.

- On the "back matter" tab, click on the "plus +" sign to edit the back matter related items on the drop-down menu. These include providing information on the Books by this Author, About the Author, Books In This Series, Praise for Author, Epilogue, Afterword, Acknowledgement and Standard Page. Select and edit the relevant items.

- The kindle create app. displays a left pane and a right pane. Actions taken on the right pane are dictated by actions taken on the left pane. The right pane contains five icons at the top which include the Print settings, Theme, Save, Preview and Publish tabs, while the left pane contains five icons which include the View, Undo, Redo, Find and Insert tabs. All these tabs are needed to create your eBook. The Print setting tab sets the book headings and interiors. The theme sets the font style. The default setting is the modern style. You can select from any of the other themes like classic, cosmos and armor. The Save tab allows the editing and formatting done on the document to be saved. The Preview tab allows you to navigate through the pages of the book. The Publish tab is the last stage of the kindle create app. Clicking the tab saves the formatted document in the folder where the original document was saved. It however, saves it in a brown-like kpf file format. So, once you are done with editing and formatting the front matter, body and back matter,

- set the Theme, Preview the document and then click "Publish".

- Then, save the formatted document as a kpf file

- Finally, go to your kdp account and upload the saved kpf file.

Exercise 3

Format your manuscript using the kindle create application tool.

4 CREATING A KINDLE DIRECT PUBLISHING ACCOUNT

Kindle direct publishing platform allows you to upload and publish your books directly and independently to the kindle store of Amazon. To successfully publish your book on Amazon, you will have to create a kdp account. Creating a kdp account involves the following steps:

i.   Go to the website kdp.amazon.com

ii. At the home screen, click on the "sign up" box

iii. Fill in your email address and a password

iv. This will lead to Two-point verification space, select "Send OTP". You will be sent a message to your phone number which contains your One Time Password (OTP)

v.   Enter the OTP, sign in and click on "kindle eBook"

vi. Fill in the information requested, scroll down and continue to the end

vii. Save and continue. This will lead you to "kindle eBook content" fill in the information requested (see below), save and continue.

viii. Click on "create your kdp account"

At the final stage of creating your kdp account, author/publisher Information, bank account details and tax information will be required.

Author/Publisher Information

Fill in the information required on your country, name, address city, state, postal code and phone number.

Bank Information

This section requires bank details which allows authors to receive electronic royalty payment. Authors without a recognized bank account should opt for check payments.

Tax Information Interview

All publishers who are not citizens of the United States must complete the U.S. tax information interview to be eligible to publish books on kdp. The Tax interview must be taken to complete the process of account creation.

Navigating the kdp platform

Working through the kdp site is made easy with the blue-font links available on the platform which serve as help guide. Authors can click on these links to get information and tips. The top pane of the kdp platform displays "Your Account", "English", "Help" and "Sign out" menu. Often when you click on your account, it will request you to enter your OTP. The next set of tabs include the "Bookshelf", "Reports", "Community" and "Marketing". The Bookshelf is the interface for authors to publish books on Amazon and all books previously published by the author are displayed in the Bookshelf. Reports tab takes you to your sales details. It displays the sales dashboard, historical sales, month-to-date e sales, payments, pre-order, promotions and others. The kdp Community interface allows interaction with other authors, gives opportunity to ask questions on the forum and gives you access to relevant e-resources. The Marketing space allows authors to enroll their eBooks in kdp select marketing program which is optional, create a campaign to promote their eBooks and paperbacks, start a kindle countdown deal and nominate eBooks for kindle deals and reading promotions.

5 UPLOADING AND PUBLISHING ON KINDLE DIRECT PUBLISHING PLATFORM

This process of publishing eBooks on Amazon Kindle Direct Publishing produces both digital publication (eBook) and paperback publication. These two types of books require a cover design which is specific for each book. The eBook has a front cover only while the paperback has a front cover, a spine and a back cover depending on the size of the pages.

A. **Uploading and publishing eBook:** To upload and publish your eBook, sign into your kdp account. Once you get to your account page, follow the steps below:

- click on the "Bookshelf" tab on the menu bar. The bookshelf is the interface for publishing. It gives an overview of all the books you have published.

- click on "create kindle eBook" icon

- This will lead you through a three-step

- Step 1, fill in the eBook details which includes information on language, book title, series, edition number, author, contributors, description, publishing rights, keywords, categories, age and grade range and pre-order details. Then, save and continue. Help links appear in blue font to serve as a guide to filling each of the sections.

- Step 2, provide the eBook content. This step allows you to upload your formatted eBook manuscript, create your eBook cover and preview your eBook.

Note that kindle eBook ISBN is not required for uploading and publishing eBooks. Creation of your eBook cover can be done using the "launch cover" icon or by uploading a design of your choice.

- Step 3, This is the eBook pricing stage. At this stage, you choose options for the kdp enrollment, territories, royalty, pricing and book lending. Notes are available in blue links as a guide for selecting the propriate option.

- Agree to the terms and conditions

- Finally, click on "Publish your kindle eBook" icon

Once published, your eBook comes alive within 72 hours.

B. Uploading and publishing paperback:

Once you get to your account page, follow the steps below:

- click on the "Bookshelf"

- click on "create paperback" icon

- This will lead you through a three-step as done for eBook creation.

- Step 1, fill in the paperback details which includes information on language, book title, series, edition number, author, contributors, description, publishing rights, keywords, categories, age and grade range and pre-order details. Then, save and continue. Help links appear in blue font to serve as a guide to filling each of the sections.

Step 2, provide the paperback content. This step allows you to upload your formatted paperback manuscript, create your paperback covers, upload author's image to back cover, preview your paperback and get an ISBN. The ISBN can either be procured from your country or a request made for a free ISBN. Building your paperback covers can be done using the "launch cover" icon or by uploading a design of your choice. Note that paperback covers include the front cover, back cover and spine depending on the size of the pages. Contents on the covers can be edited and suitable font style, font size and font color can be selected.

- Step 3, This is the paperback pricing stage. At this stage, you choose options for the kdp enrollment, territories, royalty, pricing and book lending. Notes are available in blue links as a guide for selecting the propriate option.

- Agree to the terms and conditions

- Finally, click on "Publish your paperback" icon

Once published, your eBook comes alive within 72 hours. After your book comes alive! on Amazon book store, the link to your book can be copied directly from the main site (Amazon.com). To copy the book link,

- Go to Amazon.com,

- click the three stokes top left, scroll down to click book.
- Type your book title/name on the search menu. This brings up series of books with similar titles.
- Click on your book, Open the book page
- Copy the link

Learners' guide to eBook Publishing

Ronke Aderinboye